# Cooper

**by Iain Gray**

**WRITING *to* REMEMBER**

79 Main Street, Newtongrange,
Midlothian EH22 4NA
Tel: 0131 344 0414
E-mail: info@lang-syne.co.uk
www.langsyneshop.co.uk

Design by Dorothy Meikle
Printed by Printwell Ltd
© Lang Syne Publishers Ltd 2023

All rights reserved. No part of this publication may be reproduced, stored or introduced into a retrieval system, or transmitted in any form or by any means (electronic, mechanical, photocopying, recording or otherwise) without the prior written permission of Lang Syne Publishers Ltd.

ISBN 978-1-85217-585-6

# Cooper

**MOTTO:**
By fidelity and fortitude.

**CREST:**
A lion grasping a branch of laurel.

**NAME** variations include:
- Coupar
- Couper
- Cowper

*Chapter one:*

# The origins of popular surnames

by George Forbes and Iain Gray

***If you don't know where you came from, you won't know where you're going** is a frequently quoted observation and one that has a particular resonance today when there has been a marked upsurge in interest in genealogy, with increasing numbers of people curious to trace their family roots.*

Main sources for genealogical research include census returns and official records of births, marriages and deaths – and the key to unlocking the detail they contain is obviously a family surname, one that has been 'inherited' and passed from generation to generation.

No matter our station in life, we all have a surname – but it was not until about the middle of the fourteenth century that the practice of being identified by a particular surname became commonly established throughout the British Isles.

Previous to this, it was normal for a person to be identified through the use of only a forename.

But as population gradually increased and there were many more people with the same forename, surnames were adopted to distinguish one person, or community, from another.

Many common English surnames are patronymic in origin, meaning they stem from the forename of one's father – with 'Johnson,' for example, indicating 'son of John.'

It was the Normans, in the wake of their eleventh century conquest of Anglo-Saxon England, a pivotal moment in the nation's history, who first brought surnames into usage – although it was a gradual process.

For the Normans, these were names initially based on the title of their estates, local villages and chateaux in France to distinguish and identify these landholdings.

Such grand descriptions also helped enhance the prestige of these warlords and generally glorify their lofty positions high above the humble serfs slaving away below in the pecking order who had only single names, often with Biblical connotations as in Pierre and Jacques.

The only descriptive distinctions among the peasantry concerned their occupations, like 'Pierre the swineherd' or 'Jacques the ferryman.'

Roots of surnames that came into usage in England not only included Norman-French, but also Old French, Old Norse, Old English, Middle English, German, Latin, Greek, Hebrew and the Gaelic languages of the Celts.

The Normans themselves were originally Vikings, or 'Northmen', who raided, colonised and eventually settled down around the French coastline.

They had sailed up the Seine in their long-boats in 900AD under their ferocious leader Rollo and ruled the roost in north eastern France before sailing over to conquer England in 1066 under Duke William of Normandy – better known to posterity as William the Conqueror, or King William I of England.

Granted lands in the newly-conquered England, some of their descendants later acquired territories in Wales, Scotland and Ireland – taking not only their own surnames, but also the practice of adopting a surname, with them.

But it was in England where Norman rule and custom first impacted, particularly in relation to the adoption of surnames.

This is reflected in the famous *Domesday Book*, a massive survey of much of England and Wales, ordered by William I, to determine who owned what, what it was worth and therefore how much they were liable to pay in taxes to the voracious Royal Exchequer.

Completed in 1086 and now held in the National Archives in Kew, London, 'Domesday' was an Old English word meaning 'Day of Judgement.'

This was because, in the words of one contemporary chronicler, "its decisions, like those of the Last Judgement, are unalterable."

It had been a requirement of all those English landholders – from the richest to the poorest – that they identify themselves for the purposes of the survey and for future reference by means of a surname.

This is why the *Domesday Book*, although written in Latin as was the practice for several centuries with both civic and ecclesiastical records, is an invaluable source for the early appearance of a wide range of English surnames.

Several of these names were coined in connection with occupations.

These include Baker and Smith, while Cooks, Chamberlains, Constables and Porters were to be found carrying out duties in large medieval households.

The church's influence can be found in names such as Bishop, Friar and Monk while the popular name of Bennett derives from the late fifth to mid-sixth century Saint Benedict, founder of the Benedictine order of monks.

The early medical profession is represented by Barber, while businessmen produced names that include Merchant and Sellers.

Down at the village watermill, the names that cropped up included Millar/Miller, Walker and Fuller, while other self-explanatory trades included Cooper, Tailor, Mason and Wright.

Even the scenery was utilised as in Moor, Hill, Wood and Forrest – while the hunt and the chase supplied names that include Hunter, Falconer, Fowler and Fox.

Colours are also a source of popular surnames, as in Black, Brown, Gray/Grey, Green and White, and would have denoted the colour of the clothing the person habitually wore or, apart from the obvious exception of 'Green', one's hair colouring or even complexion.

The surname Red developed into Reid, while

Blue was rare and no-one wanted to be associated with yellow.

Rather self-important individuals took surnames that include Goodman and Wiseman, while physical attributes crept into surnames such as Small and Little.

Many families proudly boast the heraldic device known as a Coat of Arms, as featured on our front cover.

The central motif of the Coat of Arms would originally have been what was borne on the shield of a warrior to distinguish himself from others on the battlefield.

Not featured on the Coat of Arms, but highlighted on page three, is the family motto and related crest – with the latter frequently different from the central motif.

Adding further variety to the rich cultural heritage that is represented by surnames is the appearance in recent times in lists of the 100 most common names found in England of ones that include Khan, Patel and Singh – names that have proud roots in the vast sub-continent of India.

Echoes of a far distant past can still be found in our surnames and they can be borne with pride in commemoration of our forebears.

*Chapter two:*

# Ancient roots

**An occupational surname, 'Cooper' originally referred to someone involved in the important trade of 'cooperage' – the making and repairing of wooden staved vessels, bound with iron hoops, such as casks, barrels, butter churns and tubs.**

Derived from the Middle Low German 'kuper' and the Middle English 'couper', it has been present on British shores from the earliest times.

In common with many other names, it became popularised as a surname in the wake of the Norman Conquest of 1066 – although the ancestors of those who would come to bear it were present in England for a considerable period before this date.

This means that flowing through the veins of many bearers of the name today may well be the blood of those Germanic tribes who invaded and settled in the south and east of the island of Britain from about the early fifth century.

Known as the Anglo-Saxons, they were composed of the Jutes, from the area of the Jutland Peninsula in modern Denmark, the Saxons from

Lower Saxony, in modern Germany and the Angles from the Angeln area of Germany.

It was the Angles who gave the name 'Engla land', or 'Aengla land' – better known as 'England.'

They held sway in what became England from approximately 550 until the Norman Conquest – when Harold II, the last of the Anglo-Saxon kings, was killed at the battle of Hastings by a mighty force led by Duke William of Normandy.

William was declared King of England on December 25, and the complete subjugation of his Anglo-Saxon subjects followed.

Those Normans who had fought on his behalf were rewarded with the lands of Anglo-Saxons, many of whom sought exile abroad as mercenaries.

Within an astonishingly short space of time, Norman manners, customs and law were imposed on England – laying the basis for what subsequently became established 'English' custom and practice.

But beneath the surface, old Anglo-Saxon culture was not totally eradicated, with some aspects absorbed into those of the Normans, while faint echoes of the Anglo-Saxon past is still seen today in the form of popular surnames such as Cooper.

A Robert le Cupere is recorded in Surrey in

1176, Selide le Copere in Norfolk in 1181 and William le Coupere in Sussex in 1296 – and it is this latter county, along with East Dorset, with which the Coopers are particularly associated.

Bearers of the name have stamped a significant mark on the historical record – not least an aristocratic dynasty that began with Anthony Ashley Cooper, 1st Earl of Shaftesbury.

Born in 1621 in the home of his maternal grandfather at Wimborne St Giles, East Dorset, and the son of Sir John Cooper, 1st Baronet, of Rockbourne, Hampshire, he was orphaned when aged eight.

Raised by a number of guardians, he was educated at Exeter College, Oxford, before studying law at Lincoln's Inn.

Marrying a daughter of Thomas Coventry, 1st Baron Coventry, in 1639, he soon became embroiled in the English Civil War.

Charles I had incurred the wrath of Parliament by his insistence on the 'divine right' of monarchs, and added to this was Parliament's fear of Catholic 'subversion' against the state and the king's stubborn refusal to grant demands for religious and constitutional concessions.

Matters came to a head with the outbreak of the civil war in 1642, with Parliamentary forces, known as the New Model Army and commanded by Oliver Cromwell and Sir Thomas Fairfax, arrayed against the Royalist army of the king.

In what became an increasingly bloody and complex conflict, spreading to Scotland and Ireland and with rapidly shifting loyalties on both sides, the king was eventually captured and executed in January of 1649 on the orders of Parliament.

Cooper, future 1st Earl of Shaftesbury, first fought as a Royalist until switching allegiance to the Parliamentary side in 1644 and later serving on England's Council of State.

But he became increasingly disaffected by the attempt of the New Model Army to govern the country following the downfall in May of 1657 of Oliver Cromwell's son and successor, Richard Cromwell.

Accordingly, he served as a member of the Convention Parliament of 1660 that resolved to restore the monarchy and was one of the members of the parliament who travelled to Charles II's court-in-exile in the Dutch republic to formally invite him to return to England and take up the throne of his late father.

Following the Restoration of Charles II, Cooper served for a time as Chancellor of the Exchequer and, in 1672, was created Earl of Shaftesbury.

A patron of the English liberal philosopher John Locke, it was in his capacity as one of what were known as The Proprietors of the Province of Carolina, in America, that he and Locke collaborated on drawing up the *Fundamental Constitutions of Carolina*.

But these were still extremely troubled political and religious times, and by 1673 he was among those who expressed concern that the heir to the throne, James, Duke of York, was secretly a Roman Catholic.

Plotting against the future monarch, the earl was forced to flee abroad, eventually settling in Rotterdam, where he died in 1683.

Portrayed on screen in the 1969 film *The First Churchills* and the 2003 BBC television mini-series *Charles II: The Power and the Passion*, the Cooper River and the Ashley River in present day South Carolina are named in his honour.

*Chapter three:*

# Honours and distinction

**Many earls of Shaftesbury have borne the name 'Anthony Ashley Cooper', sometimes hyphenated as 'Ashley-Cooper.'**

Anthony Ashley-Cooper, 2nd Earl of Shaftesbury, born in 1652 and who died in 1699, was the father through his marriage to Lady Dorothy Manners, daughter of the 8th Earl of Rutland, of the politician, philosopher and writer Anthony Ashely Cooper, 3rd Earl of Shaftesbury.

Born in 1671, much of his early education was entrusted to his grandfather's trusted friend John Locke.

Active in the politics of the Whig Party, his many philosophical works include his 1709 *Essay on the Freedom of Wit and Humour*, while he built the folly on the Shaftesbury estate at Wimborne St Giles known as the Philosopher's Tower – visible today from the B3078, south of Cranborne.

He died in 1713, while his son Anthony Ashely Cooper, 4th Earl of Shaftesbury, born in 1711, served as one of the trustees for the Establishment of the Colony of Georgia; also elected a Fellow of the scientific think-tank known as the Royal Society, he died in 1771.

In the nineteenth century, Anthony Ashley Cooper, 7th Earl of Shaftesbury, was the politician, philanthropist and great social reformer born in 1801.

Shocked by what he witnessed as a member of a special parliamentary committee that investigated the treatment of paupers and lunatics – as the poor and the mentally ill were then described – he subsequently was instrumental in the introduction of pioneering legislation that included the *County Lunatic Asylums (England) Act* of 1828 and, in the same year, the *Madhouses Act*.

A driving force behind factory reform, it was through his efforts that the *Ten Hours Act*, limiting the hours worked by children, was passed in 1847, while he was also instrumental in the introduction of legislation to improve the lot of chimney sweeps and also women and children who toiled in the deep, dark and dangerous depths of coalmines.

Also responsible for what were known as Ragged Schools – schools for poor children run by volunteers – he died in 1885, while the Shaftesbury

Memorial in Piccadilly Circus, London, commemorates his many philanthropic works.

From the nineteenth century to the twentieth, one particularly colourful – but ultimately tragic – bearer of the Shaftesbury title was the 10th earl, Anthony Ashley-Cooper.

Born in 1938 and fondly known as 'Atty' to his friends and family, his philanthropic works included serving as president of the Shaftesbury Society, formerly known as the Ragged Schools that had been formed by the 7th earl and, from 2007, known as *Livability* following its merger with another charitable institution.

A dedicated conservationist, he planted more than one million trees on his 9,000-acre estate at Wimborne St Giles in Dorset, and also served as president of the Hawk and Owl Trust and vice-president of Sir David Attenborough's British Butterfly Conservation Society.

Joint winner in 1992 of the Royal Forestry Society's National Duke of Cornwall Award for Forestry and Conservation, he was also owner of Lough Neagh, the largest freshwater lake in the British Isles and which provides 40% of Northern Ireland's drinking water.

Despite the money he and his family could have accrued from their ownership of the lake and its use, he insisted that the drinking water be extracted at no charge to the relevant Northern Irish authorities.

A flamboyant character, his preference was for ladies of foreign extraction – even as a student at Eton, in an article he penned for the college magazine, describing English debutantes as "round-shouldered, unsophisticated garglers of pink champagne".

Married three times, his first was to Italian-born Bianca de Paolis and his second to Swedish-born Christina Eva Montan.

His final, and fatal, marriage was in November of 2002 to Jamilia Ben M'Barek, born in Paris in 1961 to a Tunisian mother and Moroccan father.

The couple separated in April of 2004, and the earl focussed his attentions on another lady whom he had met in a club in Cannes and, according to sources, planned to marry after divorcing his third wife.

It was in November of 2004 that the earl mysteriously disappeared while in the French Riviera – and, following an extensive international police investigation, his remains were found about five months later at the bottom of a remote ravine in the foothills of the French Alps.

It subsequently emerged that he had been murdered, with the knowledge of his wife, by his brother-in-law Mohamed M'Barek following an argument over his plans for divorce.

Convicted of his murder, his wife and brother-in-law were sentenced by a French court to 25 years imprisonment – with his wife's later reduced to 20 years.

The earl was succeeded in the title by Anthony Ashley Cooper, 11th Earl of Shaftesbury; he died shortly after inheriting the title and it devolved, as 12th Earl of Shaftesbury, to his brother Nicholas Edmund Ashley-Cooper, born in 1979 and also known as Nick Ashley-Cooper.

Not only a prominent British Conservative party politician but also a diplomat and author, Alfred Duff Cooper, better known as Duff Cooper and ennobled as 1st Viscount Norwich, was born in 1890.

The son of Sir Alfred Cooper, a renowned doctor to the aristocracy and other members of high society, and Lady Agnes Duff, daughter of the 5th Earl of Fife, he held a number of high level government positions.

These included Financial Secretary to the War Office in 1931, Financial Secretary to the Treasury in 1934 and War Secretary in 1935.

Appointed First Lord of the Admiralty in 1937, he resigned from Parliament in 1938 over the Munich Agreement – Prime Minister Neville Chamberlain's controversial 'appeasement policy' with Nazi leader Adolf Hitler.

Later re-entering the government for a time as Minister of Information under the great wartime leader Winston Churchill, he also served as British Ambassador to France and British liaison to the Free French.

Knighted in 1947, as a man of letters he wrote what is regarded as the classic autobiography, *Old Men Forget*, while two years before his death in 1954 he was further elevated in the Peerage as Viscount Norwich, in recognition of his distinguished political and literary career.

The prestigious British literary award the Duff Cooper Prize was established in his name in 2010.

It was in 1919 that he had married the particularly feisty and grandly named Lady Diana Olivia Winifred Maud Manners, later better known as Lady Diana Cooper.

Born in 1892, she was 'officially' the daughter of the 8th Duke of Rutland – but in reality her father was the writer Henry Cust, as the result of a romantic liaison between Cust and her mother, Violet Lindsay.

Regarded as one of the great beauties of her age, it was as a member of the exclusive coterie of 'bright young things' known as The Coterie that she met her future husband.

A prolific author and commentator on social affairs, her many works include her three volumes of memoirs – *The Rainbow Comes and Goes*, *The Light of Common Day* and *Trumpets from the Sleep*.

Following her husband's elevation to the peerage as Viscount Norwich, she refused to be called 'Lady Norwich' – on the grounds that it 'sounded too much like porridge' – and took out a newspaper advertisement stating she wanted to be known as 'Lady Diana Cooper.'

She died in 1986, while her son John Julius Norwich, born in 1929, is the writer whose works include a collection of his father's diaries, *The Duff Cooper Diaries: 1915-1951*.

One of her granddaughters is the writer

Artemis Cooper, whose books include *Durable Fire: The Letters of Duff and Diana Cooper, 1913-1950*.

In contemporary British politics, Yvette Cooper, born in Inverness in 1969, has held a number of government posts that include, from 2008 to 2010, Chief Secretary to the Treasury and then as Secretary of State for Work and Pensions.

Appointed Labour Shadow Home Secretary in 2011, it was three years before this that she married fellow Labour politician Ed Balls, who was appointed Shadow Chancellor of the Exchequer in 2011.

*Chapter four:*

# On the world stage

**The son of English immigrants to the United States, Frank James Cooper was the Hollywood film legend better known as Gary Cooper.**

Born in 1901 in Helena, Montana, his father – originally from Houghton Regis, Bedfordshire – was a farmer, but later became a lawyer and judge.

Along with a brother, Cooper was sent to England to be educated for a time at Dunstable Grammar School, Bedfordshire; returning to America to continue his education, he later managed the family ranch before moving with his family from Montana to Los Angeles.

A succession of jobs followed, including a salesman for electrical signs and a promoter for a local photographer, before finding work in 1925 as a film extra.

Changing his first name to Gary on the advice of a casting director, he went on to appear in more than 100 films, winning an Academy Award for Best Actor in 1942 for his role of the title character in *Sergeant York*, and another ten years later for his role of Marshall Will Kane in *High Noon* – widely regarded as his finest role.

Also the recipient of three other Academy Award nominations, other major film credits include the 1939 *Mr Deeds Goes to Town*, the 1943 *For Whom the Bell Tolls*, the 1949 *The Fountainhead* and, from 1956, *Friendly Persuasion*.

Married to the socialite and actress Veronica Balfe – better known as 'Rocky' and whose screen name was Sandra Shaw – he also had affairs before his conversion to Catholicism with a number of co-stars who included Marlene Dietrich, Tallulah Bankhead, Grace Kelly and Patricia Neal.

He died in 1961, and is the recipient of a star on the Hollywood Walk of Fame and an inductee of the Western Performers Hall of Fame at the National Cowboy and Western Heritage Museum in Oklahoma City, while in 2009 he was featured on a commemorative U.S. postage stamp.

In the world of contemporary television and film, **Bradley Cooper** is the American actor of Irish and Italian descent born in 1975 in Philadelphia, Pennsylvania.

His many television credits include *Alias*, *Jack & Bobby* and *Nip/Tuck*, while big screen credits include, from 2009 to 2013, *The Hangover* trilogy of films, the 2011 *Limitless*, the 2012 *Silver Linings Playbook* – which won him an Academy Award nomination for Best Actor – and, from 2013, *The Place Beyond the Pines*.

Born in 1952 in Boston, **Marianne Leone Cooper** is the actress best known for her role from 2002 to 2007 of Christopher Moltisanti's mother in the popular television series *The Sopranos*.

Married to the actor Chris Cooper, her big screen credits include the 1988 *The Thin Blue Line*, the 1990 *Goodfellas* and, from 2012, *The Three Stooges*.

Starring in twenty eight films between 1930 and 1941, **Richard Cooper** was the English actor born in 1893 in Harrow-on-the Hill.

Known for his role of Captain Hastings in a series of *Hercule Poirot* films in the 1930s, other screen credits include the 1939 *Shipyard Sally* and the 1947 *Inspector Hornliegh Goes To It*; he died in 1953.

Behind the camera lens, **Kyle Cooper**, born in 1962, is the acclaimed American designer of motion picture title sequences. His many credits include the 1994 *Immortal Beloved*, the 1997

*Flubber*, the 2008 *The Incredible Hulk* and, from 2011, *American Horror Story*.

Regarded, along with Morecambe and Wise, as having been one of Britain's greatest ever comedy acts, **Tommy Cooper** was the comedian and magician born Thomas Frederick Cooper in Caerphilly, South Wales, in 1921.

He was aged eight when an aunt bought him a magic set, and he became immersed in not only mastering but also perfecting its tricks.

Serving for a time during the Second World War in North Africa with General Bernard "Monty" Montgomery's Desert Rats, he was then assigned to a NAAFI (Navy, Army and Air Force Institutes) entertainment party.

It was while performing before troops in Cairo that he first adopted his 'trademark' headgear of a fez. This was when, to the great amusement of his audience, he borrowed a passing waiter's fez after having forgotten to bring the pith helmet he normally wore as part of his act.

Developing his conjuring skills and comedy act after the war – an act that involved deliberately 'failed' tricks – he became a highly popular star of the theatre, stage and television.

A member of the exclusive magicians' club The Magic Circle, it was in April of 1984, midway through a live screening of a London Weekend Television variety show that he collapsed and died on stage.

A statue to him was unveiled in his home town of Caerphilly in 2008 by the Welsh actor Sir Anthony Hopkins, patron of The Tommy Cooper Society.

From the stage to the world of music, Vincent Damon Furnier is the veteran American rock star better known as **Alice Cooper** – the name of the band he formed in the late 1960s.

Born in Detroit, Michigan, in 1948, the son of a lay preacher, he enjoyed hit singles with his band that include the 1972 *School's Out* and albums that include the 1973 *Billion Dollar Babies*.

As a solo artist, he has enjoyed success with albums that include his 1975 *Welcome to My Nightmare*, the 1977 *Lace and Whiskey* and the 1983 *DaDa*.

Known as a master of the rock genre known as 'shock rock', utilising stage props that have ranged from a boa constrictor to guillotines and electric chairs, rather more conventionally he is also a golfing celebrity.

Born in 1942 in Watford, Hertfordshire, **Ray Cooper** is the English percussionist who has worked with a range of artists who include George Harrison, Eric Clapton, Elton John and Billy Joel.

Bearers of the Cooper name have also excelled in the highly competitive world of sport.

In the boxing ring, **Henry Cooper** was the English heavyweight champion known fondly to boxing fans in particular and the public in general as "Our 'Enery."

Born in 1934 in Lambeth, London, along with his identical twin George – who boxed as Jim Cooper – and elder brother Bern, he was involved in sport from an early age.

Starting his boxing career in 1949 with the Eltham Amateur Boxing Club, he served his National Service in the Royal Army Ordnance Corps, where he was recruited for his boxing skills and make a name for himself with his deadly left hook known as 'Enry's 'Ammer'.

Turning professional, he went on to hold the British, Commonwealth and European heavyweight titles – while most famously in a non-professional fight in 1963 unsuccessfully challenging American boxer Cassius Clay, later known as Mohammed Ali, but nevertheless felling him to the canvas with his 'Enery's Ammer.'

The two boxers were matched again in 1966, with Ali retaining his heavyweight title after Cooper suffered a technical knockout.

Winner, in 1967, of the BBC Sports Personality of the Year Award and the winner again in 1970, he died in 2011.

The only British boxer to have won three prestigious Lonsdale Belts outright, he was also a recipient before his death of an OBE in 1969 and a knighthood in 2000 as Sir Henry Cooper.

On the fields of European football, David Cooper, better known as **Davie Cooper**, was the Scottish player born in Hamilton, South Lanarkshire, in 1956.

Having played for Clydebank, Rangers and Motherwell and the Scotland national team, he died in 1995 after suffering a brain haemorrhage while he and fellow Scottish international Charlie Nicholas were recording a coaching film for young players.

Highly respected by all football fans, regardless of their club allegiance, Motherwell's Fir Park stadium North Stand was named in his honour after his death as the Davie Cooper Stand.

An England international footballer from 1927 to 1934 and playing for teams that included Port Vale, Derby County and Liverpool, Thomas Cooper, better known as **Tom Cooper**, was born in 1904 in Stoke-on-Trent.

Serving with the Royal Military Police during the Second World War, he was killed in June of 1940 after his despatch motorcycle collided with a lorry; an inquiry into the accident led to the order that in future all despatch riders must wear a crash helmet.

On the rugby pitch, **Gareth Cooper**, born in Bridgend in 1979, is the Welsh former rugby union scrum-half who, in addition to representing his nation at international level, played for teams that include Pencoed, Bath, Celtic Dragons, Newport Gwent Dragons, Gloucester and the Cardiff Blues.

From the rough and tumble of rugby to tennis, **Ashley Cooper** is the Australian former player who in 1958 became one of only ten men – as of 2014 – to win three of the four Grand Slam events in the same year – winning the singles at the Australian, American and British championships.

Born in Melbourne in 1936, he is an inductee of both the Sport Australia Hall of Fame and the International Tennis Hall of Fame, while in 2007 he was appointed an Officer of the Order of Australia for his service to tennis.

Bearers of the proud name of Cooper have also excelled in the highly creative world of art.

Born in London in 1609, Abraham Alexander Cooper, better known as **Alexander Cooper**, was the English painter considered the best portrait miniaturist of his time.

Having carried out commissions for members of European royalty who included Christina, Queen Regant of Sweden, Christian IV of Denmark and Prince Rupert of the Rhine, he died in 1660.

He was a brother of the English miniature painter **Samuel Cooper**, one of whose works include a portrait of the wife of celebrated diarist Samuel Pepys; he died in 1672.

Still in the artistic world, **Alfred Heaton Cooper**, born in Manchester in 1863, was the acclaimed Victorian landscape painter particularly renowned for his landscapes of the grandeur of the Lake District, where he died in 1929.

Bearers of the name have also stamped a mark on the historical record through their pioneering work in the sciences.

Born in New York City in 1930, **Leon N.**

**Cooper** is the American physicist who, along with John Bardeen and John Robert Schrieffer, shared the Nobel Prize for physics in 1972 for their work on a special theory of superconductivity.

A Fellow of the American Physical Society and the American Academy of Arts and Sciences, the character of Sheldon Cooper in the popular television comedy series *The Big Bang Theory* is named in part after him.